Hawaii Bingo Book

A COMPLETE BINGO GAME IN A BOOK

Written By Rebecca Stark

ISBN 978-0-87386-504-3

Educational Books 'n' Bingo

Printed in the United States of America.

DIRECTIONS

INCLUDED:

List of Terms

Templates for Additional Terms and Clues

2 Clues per Term

30 Unique Bingo Cards

Markers

1. **Either cut apart the book or make copies of ALL the sheets. You might want to make an extra copy of the clue sheets to use for introduction and review. Keep the sheets in an envelope for easy reuse.**

2. Cut apart the call cards with terms and clues.

3. Pass out one bingo card per student. There are enough for a class of 30.

4. Pass out markers. You may cut apart the markers included in this book or use any other small items of your choice.

5. Decide whether or not you will require the entire card to be filled. Requiring the entire card to be filled provides a better review. However, if you have a short time to fill, you may prefer to have them do the just the border or some other format. Tell the class before you begin what is required.

6. There are 50 terms. Read the list before you begin. If there are any terms that have not been covered in class, you may want to read to the students the term and clues before you begin.

7. There is a blank space in the middle of each card. You can instruct the students to use it as a free space or you can write in answers to cover terms not included. Of course, in this case you would create your own clues. (Templates provided.)

8. Shuffle the cards and place them in a pile. Two or three clues are provided for each term. If you plan to play the game with the same group more than once, you might want to choose a different clue for each game. If not, you may choose to use more than one clue.

9. Be sure to keep the cards you have used for the present game in a separate pile. When a student calls, "Bingo," he or she will have to verify that the correct answers are on his or her card AND that the markers were placed in response to the proper questions. Pull out the cards that are on the student's card keeping them in the order they were used in the game. Read each clue as it was given and ask the student to identify the correct answer from his or her card.

10. If the student has the correct answers on the card AND has shown that they were marked in response to the *correct questions,* then that student is the winner and the game is over. If the student does not have the correct answers on the card OR he or she marked the answers in response to *the wrong questions,* then the game continues until there is a proper winner.

11. If you want to play again, reshuffle the cards and begin again.

Have fun!

TERMS INCLUDED

Agricultural	Lei
Archipelago	Queen Liliuokalani
Black Coral(s)	Maui
Captain James Cook	Mauna Kea
Channel	Molokai
Color	Monk Seal(s)
Counties	Motto
Diamond Head	Nene
Earthquakes	Nickname
Fish	Niihau
Flag	Oahu
Great Seal	Pacific Ocean
Hawaii	Pearl Harbor
Hawaiians	Pineapple
Hilo	Pua Aloalo
Honolulu	Pulelehua
Hula	Song
Humpback Whale(s)	Sport
Islands	Trigger Fish
Kauai	Tsunami
Kiluaea	Volcanoes
King Kamehameha I	Union
Kukui	USS Arizona
Lanai	Waikiki
Language	Wailuku

Additional Terms

Choose as many additional terms as you would like and write them in the squares. Repeat each as desired.
Cut out the squares and randomly distribute them to the class.
Instruct the students to place their square on the center space of their card.

Hawaii Bingo

Clues for Additional Terms

Write three clues for each of your additional terms.

_____	_____
1.	1.
2.	2.
3.	3.
_____	_____
1.	1.
2.	2.
3.	3.
_____	_____
1.	1.
2.	2.
3.	3.

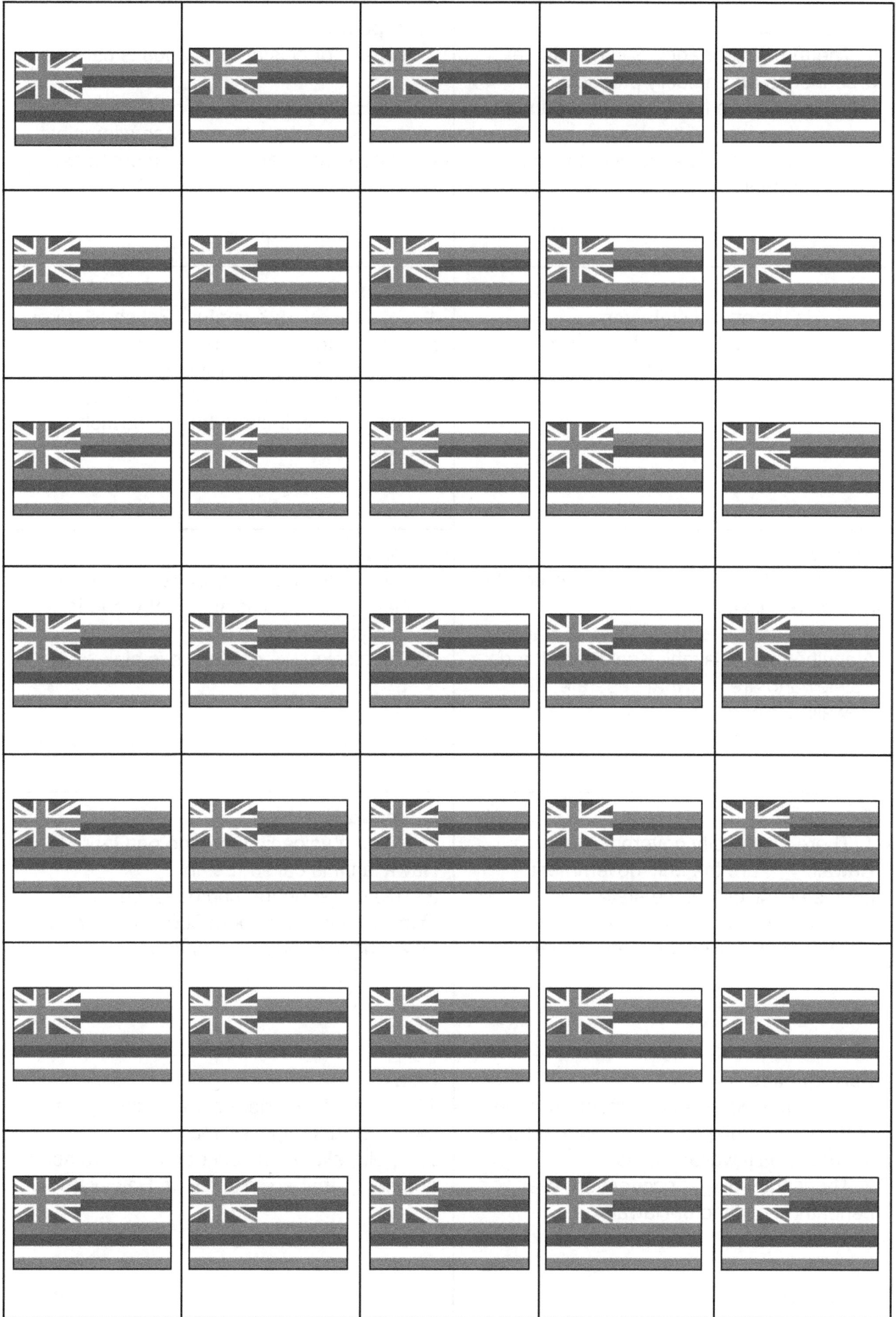

Agricultural 1. The most important ___ products are greenhouse and nursery products, pineapples, cane for sugar, macadamia nuts, and coffee. 2. Beef cattle, dairy, eggs and hogs are also important ___ products.	**Archipelago** 1. A chain, or cluster, of islands is called an ___. 2. The Hawaiian ___ comprises eight major islands, several atolls, many smaller islets, and undersea seamounts, or mountains.
Black Coral(s) 1. ___ is the official state gem. 2. ___ are actually animals that live in colonies. ___ is often made into jewelry.	**Captain James Cook** 1. ___ was an 18th-century British explorer, navigator, and cartographer. 2. ___ was the first European to make contact with the Hawaiian Islands. He named the archipelago the "Sandwich Islands."
Channel 1. In an archipelago the water between the islands is called a ___. 2. Kaiwi, Auau, Kalohi, Alalakeiki, Pailolo, Alenuihaha, Kaulakahi, Kealaikahiki and Kaieiewaho are ___ that separate the Hawaiian islands.	**Color** 1. Each of the 8 main islands has a different official ___ . The official ___ of Oahu is is golden yellow. 2. The official ___ of Maui is is pink.
Counties 1. There are no city governments in Hawaii. ___ are the only government bodies below that of the state. 2. There are five ___ in Hawaii: Hawaii, Maui, Kalawao, Honolulu, and Kauai.	**Diamond Head** 1. ___ is a volcanic tuff cone on Oahu. In Hawaiian it is called "Le'ahi." 2. This crater on the southeast coast of Oahu was formed about 300,000 years ago by a single, explosive eruption.
Earthquakes 1. ___ and volcanoes are important parts of the island-building processes that have shaped the Hawaiian Islands. 2. Thousands of ___ occur every year beneath the Island of Hawaii.	**Fish** 1. The most important commercial ___ are swordfish and bigeye tuna. 2. Opelu, akule, ahi, aku, and moi are some of the ___ that are plentiful in Hawaiian waters.

Flag 1. The state ___ was adopted in 1816. It has served as the ___ of the kingdom, the republic, the territory, and the state of Hawaii. 2. The state ___ contains the Union Jack of Great Britain.	**Great Seal** 1. The ___ features King Kamehameha I holding his staff and Liberty holding the Hawaiian flag on either side of the heraldic shield. A Phoenix rises up from native foliage. 2. The Great ___ also contains the year 1959, the year of statehood, and the state motto.
Hawaii 1. Also called The Big Island, ___ is the largest island in the United States. 2. This island was formed by five volcanoes, two of which are still active. The highest point in the state is on this island.	**Hawaiians** 1. People who are native to Hawaii are called ___. 2. People who are not native ___, even if born in the state, are referred to as Hawaii residents or islanders. They are not called ___.
Hilo 1. ___ is the county seat of the County of Hawaii. 2. ___ Bay is situated upon two shield volcanoes: Mauna Loa, an active volcano, and Mauna Kea, a dormant volcano.	**Honolulu** 1. ___ is the capital and most populous city of the state of Hawaii. 2. According to the 2010 census, ___ is the most populous state capital relative to state population.
Hula 1. The ___ is the official state dance. 2. ___ is an integrated system of poetry, movement and rhythm. Every movement has a specific meaning.	**Humpback Whale(s)** 1. The ___ is the official marine mammal. 2. ___ spend the Northern Hemisphere's winter months in the protected waters of the Auau Channel.
Islands 1. Hawaii is the only state made up entirely of ___. 2. The 8 main ___ are Hawaii, Maui, Oahu, Kauai, Molokai, Lanai, Niihau, and Kahoolawe. Kahoolawe is not inhabited. Hawaii Bingo	**Kauai** 1. ___ is geologically the oldest and northernmost of the main Hawaiian Islands. 2. The Napali Coast, Hanalei Bay, and the Waimea Canyon are in ___.

Kiluaea
1. ____ may be the world's most active volcano.
2. ____ is the youngest and southeastern-most volcano on the Big Island of Hawaii.

King Kamehameha I
1. ____was king of the Hawaiian Islands from July 1782 until his death on May 8, 1819. He unified the Hawaiian Islands into one kingdom.
2. A statue of ____ in bronze and gold leaf by Thomas Ridgeway Gould stands across from Iolani Palace in Honolulu .

Kukui
1. The ____ tree is the official state tree. The blossom of the ____ is also the official Island flower of Molokai.
2. The ____ tree is also referred to as the candlenut tree.

Lanai
1. ____ is known as Pineapple Island because of its past as an island-wide pineapple plantation.
2. ____ City is the only town on the island of ____. The population is only about 3,100.

Language
1. Hawaiian is the native ____ of Hawaii.
2. Hawaii is the only state to have an official native ____.

Lei
1. A ____ is a garland of objects, usually flowers. Each of the 8 main islands has a different flower as its official ____ material.
2. Lokelani, also known as Damask Rose, is the official ____ material of Maui.

Queen Liliuokalani
1. ____ was the last reigning monarch of the Hawaiian islands. She reigned from 1891 to 1893.
2. During her confinement at Iolani Palace, ____ wrote one of Hawaii's most beloved songs, "Aloha Oe," or "Farewell to Thee."

Maui
1. Lahaina is on the island of ____. During the mid-1800s it was a historic whaling village.
2. The beaches of Kaanapali and Haleakala National Park on the island of ____ are popular tourist attractions.

Mauna Kea
1. At 13,796 feet above sea level, ____ is the highest point in the state.
2. ____ is a dormant volcano. It last erupted about 4,500 years ago. Its name means "White Mountain."

Molokai
1. During the 19th century, Father Damien and Mother Marianne Cope cared for sufferers of Hansen's disease on the island of ____.
2. Sufferers of Hansen's disease, or leprosy, were forced into quarantine on ____ by the Hawaiian government. There are no active cases of Hansen's disease on ____ today.

Hawaii Bingo

Monk Seal(s) 1. The Hawaiian ___ is the official mammal. ___ spend most of their time at sea, but come ashore to rest on beaches 2. The ___ is one of the nation's most threatened species. It gets its name from the folds of skin that look a little like a monk's cowl.	**Motto** 1. The state ___, *"Ua mau ke ea o ka aina i ka pono,"* was supposedly said by King Kamehameha III after a British admiral attempted a takeover in 1843. 2. In English, the state ___ is "The life of the land is perpetuated in righteousness."
Nene 1. The ___ is the state bird. 2. The ___ is also known as the Hawaiian goose. Its feet are only half as webbed as those of other geese.	**Nickname** 1. Hawaii's official ___ is "Aloha State." 2. An unofficial ___ is "Paradise of the Pacific."
Niihau 1. ___ is privately owned. It is the smallest of the habited islands. 2. ___ is nicknamed "The Forbidden Isle" because it is off-limits to all but relatives of the island's owners, U.S. Navy personnel, government officials, and invited guests.	**Oahu** 1. ___ is the third largest of the Hawaiian Islands in area and the most populous. 2. The state capital, Honolulu, is on ___'s southeast coast.
Pacific Ocean 1. Hawaii is surrounded by the ___. 2. Hawaii is located in the South ___, about 2,400 miles southwest of the continental United States.	**Pearl Harbor** 1. ___ is the largest natural harbor in the state. It is the only U.S. naval base to be recognized as a National Historical Landmark. 2. The bombing of ___ by the Japanese on December 7, 1941, brought the United States into World War II.
Pineapple 1. Hawaiian ___ plantations produce almost a third of the world's crop and supply about 60 percent of canned ___ products. 2. James Dole, commonly known as the "___ King," arrived in Hawaii in 1899. He started his first plantation in Wahiawa a year later and built a ___ cannery the following year.	**Pua Aloalo** 1. The ___ is the state flower. 2. The ___ is called the yellow hibiscus in English.

Hawaii Bingo

© Barbara M. Peller

Pulelehua
1. The ____ is the state insect.
2. The ____ is also known as the Kamehameha butterfly.

Song
1. "Hawai`i Pono`i" is the state ____ and former national anthem of Hawaii.
2. The title of the state ____ translates in English to "Hawaii's own true sons."

Sport
1. Outrigger canoe paddling is the official team ____ of Hawaii.
2. Surfing is the official individual ____ of Hawaii.

Trigger Fish
1. The rectangular ____ is the state fish.
2. In Hawaiian, the rectangular ____ is called "humuhumunukunukuapua`a." Some people joke that the name is longer than the fish.

Tsunami
1. A ____ is a great sea wave mainly associated with the occurrence of earthquakes or volcanoes beneath the sea.
2. Detecting a ____ is difficult because in the deep ocean, the ____ wave may only be a few inches high.

Volcanoes
1. Mauna Loa and Kilauea are active ____.
2. Kohala, Hualalai and Mauna Kea are dormant ____.

Union
1. Hawaii was admitted to the ____ on August 21, 1959.
2. Hawaii was the 50th state to enter the ____.

USS Arizona
1. The ____ was bombed during the Japanese attack on Pearl Harbor on December 7, 1941.
2. The wreck of the ____ lies at the bottom of Pearl Harbor. The ____ Memorial is dedicated to the 1,177 officers and crew who died during the attack.

Waikiki
1. ____ is a neighborhood of Honolulu. ____ Beach is a popular tourist destination.
2. Diamond Head is on the southeast coast of Oahu at the end of ____. It overlooks the Pacific Ocean.

Wailuku
1. The ____ River is the state's longest river.
2. The course of the ____ River lies mostly along the divide between the lava flows of Mauna Kea and Mauna Loa.

Hawaii Bingo

Hawaii Bingo

Pearl Harbor	Agricultural	Black Coral(s)	Islands	Channel
Hula	Archipelago	*USS Arizona*	Molokai	Pulelehua
Union	Mauna Kea		Niihau	Waikiki
Volcanoes	Pua Aloalo	Tsunami	Maui	Motto
Nickname	King Kamehameha I	Hawaiians	Sport	Language

Hawaii Bingo: Card No. 1

Hawaii Bingo

Volcanoes	Union	Lanai	Pineapple	Queen Liliuokalani
Motto	Hilo	Diamond Head	Pua Aloalo	Nene
Fish	King Kamehameha I		Kukui	Tsunami
Oahu	Pacific Ocean	Mauna Kea	Wailuku	Channel
Pulelehua	*USS Arizona*	Hawaiians	Hula	Sport

Hawaii Bingo

King Kamehameha I	Tsunami	Hilo	Maui	Union
Motto	Archipelago	Earthquakes	Agricultural	Kiluaea
Pua Aloalo	*USS Arizona*		Nene	Captain James Cook
Mauna Kea	Fish	Nickname	Oahu	Lanai
Sport	Flag	Hawaiians	Wailuku	Queen Liliuokalani

Hawaii Bingo

Mauna Kea	Nene	Black Coral(s)	Flag	Queen Liliuokalani
Monk Seal(s)	Counties	Agricultural	Pineapple	Union
Niihau	Oahu		Language	Islands
Tsunami	Archipelago	*USS Arizona*	Hawaiians	Diamond Head
Great Seal	Pulelehua	Color	Sport	Waikiki

Hawaii Bingo

Pulelehua	Channel	Pua Aloalo	Diamond Head	Flag
Monk Seal(s)	Tsunami	Earthquakes	Kukui	Archipelago
Black Coral(s)	Waikiki		Molokai	Kauai
Language	Queen Liliuokalani	Pearl Harbor	Wailuku	Hawaii
Hilo	Hawaiians	Union	Mauna Kea	Niihau

Hawaii Bingo: Card No. 5

Hawaii Bingo

Captain James Cook	Nene	Lanai	Queen Liliuokalani	Waikiki
Maui	Pua Aloalo	Hawaii	Agricultural	Union
Pineapple	Great Seal		Counties	Kukui
Hawaiians	Nickname	Wailuku	Color	Black Coral(s)
Motto	Diamond Head	Pearl Harbor	Niihau	Honolulu

Hawaii Bingo

Pearl Harbor	Nene	Kauai	Tsunami	Hilo
Motto	Queen Liliuokalani	King Kamehameha I	Archipelago	Monk Seal(s)
Waikiki	Islands		Kukui	Counties
Mauna Kea	Oahu	Earthquakes	Volcanoes	Fish
Hawaiians	Flag	Wailuku	Color	Captain James Cook

Hawaii Bingo

Niihau	Nene	Humpback Whale(s)	Maui	Counties
Monk Seal(s)	Black Coral(s)	Pineapple	Waikiki	Diamond Head
Honolulu	Flag		Queen Liliuokalani	Channel
Sport	Mauna Kea	Volcanoes	Great Seal	Oahu
USS Arizona	Hawaiians	Color	Pua Aloalo	Motto

Hawaii Bingo

Kukui	Hilo	King Kamehameha I	Honolulu	Flag
Great Seal	Queen Liliuokalani	Niihau	Pua Aloalo	Nene
Kiluaea	Pearl Harbor		Archipelago	Humpback Whale(s)
Hawaii	Channel	Nickname	Molokai	Kauai
Oahu	Wailuku	Earthquakes	Volcanoes	Language

Hawaii Bingo

Volcanoes	Maui	Counties	Pineapple	Honolulu
Waikiki	Diamond Head	Agricultural	Archipelago	Queen Liliuokalani
Flag	Nene		Islands	Fish
Nickname	Language	Hawaii	Wailuku	Kiluaea
Earthquakes	Motto	Lanai	Pulelehua	Niihau

Hawaii Bingo

Captain James Cook	Nene	Pua Aloalo	Hawaii	Motto
Humpback Whale(s)	Kiluaea	Molokai	Kukui	Agricultural
Monk Seal(s)	Queen Liliuokalani		Lanai	King Kamehameha I
Earthquakes	Union	Wailuku	Flag	Volcanoes
Great Seal	Hawaiians	Pearl Harbor	Color	Hilo

Hawaii Bingo

Hilo	Channel	Kiluaea	Maui	Kukui
King Kamehameha I	Motto	Black Coral(s)	Color	Archipelago
Pearl Harbor	Kauai		Waikiki	Pineapple
Hawaiians	Oahu	Queen Liliuokalani	Volcanoes	Monk Seal(s)
Nene	Humpback Whale(s)	Flag	Great Seal	Diamond Head

Hawaii Bingo: Card No. 12

Hawaii Bingo

Hawaii	Channel	Captain James Cook	Kiluaea	Waikiki
Black Coral(s)	Humpback Whale(s)	Queen Liliuokalani	Kukui	Fish
Maui	Diamond Head		King Kamehameha I	Kauai
Niihau	Wailuku	Counties	Flag	Volcanoes
Hawaiians	Language	Color	Pearl Harbor	Molokai

Hawaii Bingo

Hula	Queen Liliuokalani	Pua Aloalo	Kukui	Great Seal
Diamond Head	Pearl Harbor	Kiluaea	Archipelago	Nene
Hawaii	Islands		Lanai	Earthquakes
Language	Wailuku	Flag	Counties	Captain James Cook
Hawaiians	Pineapple	Fish	Motto	Niihau

Hawaii Bingo

Molokai	Kukui	Pua Aloalo	Hilo	Maui
Captain James Cook	Lanai	Agricultural	Black Coral(s)	Great Seal
Waikiki	Pearl Harbor		Union	Nene
Hawaiians	Kiluaea	Humpback Whale(s)	Wailuku	Hawaii
Motto	Oahu	Color	Honolulu	King Kamehameha I

Hawaii Bingo

Counties	Kiluaea	Humpback Whale(s)	Honolulu	Pacific Ocean
Pineapple	Fish	Kauai	Monk Seal(s)	Islands
Hawaii	Channel		Waikiki	King Kamehameha I
Mauna Kea	Diamond Head	Hawaiians	Molokai	Volcanoes
Great Seal	Trigger Fish	Color	Oahu	Nene

Hawaii Bingo

Earthquakes	Song	Lei	Kiluaea	Hula
Molokai	Great Seal	Wailuku	Islands	Kauai
Kukui	Niihau		Trigger Fish	Humpback Whale(s)
Language	Motto	Volcanoes	Pua Aloalo	Fish
Nickname	Hawaii	Hilo	Maui	Channel

Hawaii Bingo

Honolulu	Flag	Diamond Head	Hawaii	Pineapple
Nene	Earthquakes	Nickname	Waikiki	Great Seal
Kukui	Fish		Lei	Black Coral(s)
Channel	Agricultural	Wailuku	Volcanoes	Lanai
Trigger Fish	Kiluaea	Pua Aloalo	Song	Captain James Cook

Hawaii Bingo

Waikiki	Captain James Cook	Kiluaea	Humpback Whale(s)	Volcanoes
Molokai	Maui	Nene	Hilo	Islands
Song	Flag		Archipelago	Union
Lanai	Trigger Fish	Nickname	Oahu	Lei
Black Coral(s)	Pacific Ocean	Motto	Niihau	Color

Hawaii Bingo: Card No. 19

Hawaii Bingo

Hula	Song	Maui	Kiluaea	Color
Diamond Head	King Kamehameha I	Monk Seal(s)	Nickname	Pineapple
Channel	Kauai		Mauna Kea	Agricultural
Pulelehua	*USS Arizona*	Sport	Oahu	Trigger Fish
Tsunami	Niihau	Pacific Ocean	Volcanoes	Lei

Hawaii Bingo: Card No. 20

Hawaii Bingo

Molokai	Captain James Cook	Monk Seal(s)	Kiluaea	Pulelehua
Channel	Lei	Counties	Humpback Whale(s)	Pearl Harbor
Fish	Motto		Song	Pua Aloalo
Nickname	Hilo	Trigger Fish	Language	Niihau
Mauna Kea	Pacific Ocean	Color	Earthquakes	Oahu

Hawaii Bingo

Honolulu	Lanai	Lei	Black Coral(s)	Hawaii
Pineapple	Maui	Union	Humpback Whale(s)	Archipelago
Diamond Head	Islands		Pearl Harbor	Kauai
Trigger Fish	Language	Oahu	Agricultural	Monk Seal(s)
Pacific Ocean	Earthquakes	Song	Fish	Mauna Kea

Hawaii Bingo

Counties	Song	Hilo	Black Coral(s)	Color
Captain James Cook	Hula	Motto	Molokai	Agricultural
Lanai	Hawaii		Sport	Pearl Harbor
Fish	Pacific Ocean	Trigger Fish	Earthquakes	Oahu
Pulelehua	*USS Arizona*	Niihau	Nickname	Lei

Hawaii Bingo

Counties	Niihau	Hula	Song	Humpback Whale(s)
Lei	Color	Monk Seal(s)	Pineapple	Pearl Harbor
Kauai	Honolulu		Hawaii	Fish
Pulelehua	Sport	Trigger Fish	Earthquakes	Channel
Tsunami	Mauna Kea	Pacific Ocean	Maui	*USS Arizona*

Hawaii Bingo

Mauna Kea	Monk Seal(s)	Song	Pua Aloalo	Lei
Agricultural	Channel	Molokai	Counties	Archipelago
Language	Humpback Whale(s)		Sport	Trigger Fish
Union	Pulelehua	*USS Arizona*	Pacific Ocean	Islands
Color	Hula	Diamond Head	Great Seal	Tsunami

Hawaii Bingo: Card No. 25

Hawaii Bingo

Lei	Song	Lanai	Pineapple	Honolulu
Nickname	Maui	Humpback Whale(s)	Hula	Counties
Language	Sport		Islands	Mauna Kea
Earthquakes	Black Coral(s)	Pulelehua	Pacific Ocean	Trigger Fish
Kauai	Great Seal	Pua Aloalo	*USS Arizona*	Tsunami

Hawaii Bingo

Lanai	Diamond Head	Song	Hula	King Kamehameha I
Pulelehua	Sport	Molokai	Trigger Fish	Archipelago
Wailuku	*USS Arizona*		Pacific Ocean	Mauna Kea
Honolulu	Captain James Cook	Monk Seal(s)	Tsunami	Agricultural
Great Seal	Islands	Lei	Union	Kauai

Hawaii Bingo

Lanai	Hula	Union	Song	Counties
King Kamehameha I	Lei	Sport	Pineapple	Islands
USS Arizona	Fish		Kauai	Nickname
Volcanoes	Honolulu	Motto	Pacific Ocean	Trigger Fish
Black Coral(s)	Kukui	Great Seal	Tsunami	Pulelehua

Hawaii Bingo

Lei	Hula	Honolulu	Molokai	Kukui
Oahu	Nickname	Monk Seal(s)	Kauai	Union
Language	Sport		Archipelago	Song
King Kamehameha I	Pulelehua	Queen Liliuokalani	Pacific Ocean	Trigger Fish
Counties	Humpback Whale(s)	Tsunami	Captain James Cook	*USS Arizona*

Hawaii Bingo

Flag	Song	Pineapple	Kukui	Trigger Fish
Agricultural	Hula	Lanai	Islands	Archipelago
Language	Hawaii		Kauai	Monk Seal(s)
Tsunami	Captain James Cook	Black Coral(s)	Pacific Ocean	Sport
Pulelehua	Waikiki	*USS Arizona*	Lei	Union

Hawaii Bingo: Card No. 30

9 780873 865043